Brenda G. Martin

AF421853

The Alphabet

Learned Quickly and Easily

The Alphabet: Learned Quickly and Easily by Brenda G. Martin

Copyright © 2024 by **Brenda G. Martin**

All rights reserved. No part of this book may be reproduced, transmitted, or distributed in any form by any means, including, but not limited to, recording, photocopying, or taking screenshots of parts of the book, without prior written permission from the author or the publisher. Brief quotations for non-commercial purposes, such as book reviews, permitted by Fair Use of the U.S. Copyright Law, are allowed without written permissions, as long as such quotations do not cause damage to the book's commercial value. For permissions, write to the publisher, whose address is stated below.

E-book: 979-8-3302-7323-2
Paperback: 979-8-3302-7322-5
Hardback: 979-8-3302-7325-6

Printed in the United States of America.

Genre Library Solutions
300 Delaware Ave. Suite 210,
Wilmington, DE 19801
www.genrelibrarysolutions.com
(315) 367-7314

Here's the author's additional tips for parents and teachers:

1. Regular Short Vowel Reviews: At the start of class, allocate 5-10 minutes, 2 or 3 times a week, to review short vowels. Short vowels can be a foundational aspect of phonics instruction, and consistent review helps reinforce their sounds. Use engaging activities such as flashcards, word blending exercises, or phonics songs to ensure students are actively practicing. Focus on common short vowel sounds in CVC (consonant-vowel-consonant) words like "cat," "dog," and "pen," as this repetition will solidify students' ability to recognize and use these sounds in reading and writing.

2. Dedicated Long Vowel Review: Once a week, spend about 5 minutes reviewing long vowel sounds. Long vowels can be more complex, as they often involve silent letters or different spelling patterns (e.g., "cake," "boat," "tree"). Use this time to focus on long vowel patterns, such as vowel-consonant-silent-e (VCe) or vowel teams like "ee" and "oa." Interactive methods, like having students find long vowel words in a reading passage or using games, can make this review more engaging. Regular attention to long vowels will help students better distinguish between short and long sounds, improving their fluency and spelling.

Note: The amount of practice for each class can be adjusted to more practice or less practice as each class/students have different needs. (Sometimes the amount of practice can be adjusted by the repetitions or practice times to fit each group.)

Teachers Manual
LEARNING THE ALPHABET QUICKLY AND EASILY

Welcome to an exciting and successful way to teach the alphabet and its phonetic sounds, which are the basic foundations of learning to read. By combining multi-sensory methods (such as auditory, visual, and kinesthetic) with association memory techniques, learning is accelerated and enhanced. The senses of sight, hearing, and touch are merged with memory training to help students be more successful in reading. Reading—a complex concept— becomes easier to learn by using these techniques. Reading requires knowledge of the letters and their phonetic sounds on an automatic level and must be over-learned to be in a person's long-term memory. When a student struggles to recall the sounds for the letters, reading and spelling are hindered, and reading is less smooth. There are large numbers of adults and children who do not make all the letters' sounds correctly. This book will help them correct these common mistakes through picture association and stories.

I developed the methods in this book over the years to find the most effective ways of teaching. My classes have consisted of economically disadvantaged, special education students with dyslexia, learning disabilities, and severe learning problems, etc. Stories were composed from the unique pictures to help students visualize the letters while remembering the phonetic sounds. With the ability to see the letter inside the picture, the student knows two words beginning with that letter's sound. All the methods in this book help students know the direction of the letters, thereby decreasing reversals or flipping of letters. Visual and auditory memory improves. A difficult concept is simplified and made both fun and interesting. The letters and the sounds go along with the pictures and finally make sense. Memory is enhanced by associating the letters with the pictures and stories. Students are able to do much better because letters and their sounds are less confusing. Even the similar sounding names of these letters: B, C, D, G, P, T, V, and Z are not confused.

HOW TO USE THIS BOOK

Teachers should familiarize themselves with the Teacher/Parent Page, the Student Page, and this manual before teaching the students. After reading everything carefully, begin by looking again in detail at the Teacher/Parent Page for short a. In parenthesis are the words, "(Different Name from Sound A)". The sound the short a makes, **(ă)** is not the same sound as the actual name of the letter (a). This concept holds true for all short vowels. For all the long vowels, the name of the letter is the actual sound that the letter makes. This is the reason for the title, "(Same Name and Sound A)", one example from the book.

Have a mirror available to look at the mouth when you say the sound that each letter makes to notice how the tongue, mouth, and lips move while saying the sound. For sounds made in the throat, put your hand on the neck to feel the vibration made while making this phonetic sound. Talk about this in detail, and demonstrate each sound until the student can mimic the sound correctly. Point out how wide the mouth is open and whether the sound is made toward the front, middle, or back of the mouth. Point out if the sound is voiced or quiet. Do this consistently with each letter. Work on one letter at a time.

When teaching short vowel sounds, emphasize and exaggerate slightly that the tongue goes down when saying short vowel sounds just as something that is down is also short. This connects the word short with the tongue being down when saying short vowel sounds in isolation. Just the opposite is true of long vowels. Emphasize and exaggerate slightly that when saying long vowels that the tongue goes up slightly. Connect the word long with the idea that things that are long extend upward.

The rules concerning the number of vowels per syllable for each word example can be emphasized. Review the rule that states: "For the words with a short vowel sound, there is usually one vowel per syllable" (when they are ready). Go over the rule that states: "For words with the long vowel sound, there are usually two vowels per syllable, but the first vowel makes the long sound while the second vowel is silent." Read the examples given and include other examples that follow this rule.

Later on, as the students get better at visualization and auditory training, teachers may choose to add additional objects to the story that also begin with that particular sound. For example, while working on short a say, "Abigail watched in the afternoon as the alligator got down from the apple tree. An ant, Aunt Ann, and an antelope watched too." The list of short a things can grow. Just be sure that each word does make the correct phonetic sound for that particular phoneme.

Through the combination of association, visualization, auditory, kinesthetic, and repetition methods, learning is accelerated. Each method in isolation is not nearly as effective as each method combined. Integrating the various learning modalities helps in learning anything more quickly. Using more of the senses helps retain more of the information to be learned.

Use these techniques, and you will begin to see students of any age succeed who have not been successful. It has worked many times for my students whom, at times, I thought had little hope. They can now understand, remember, and use what they learned from this book.

STUDENT PAGES

On the student page, read or sing the story to see the relationship between the story, the letter, and the picture. The story and the picture are unique in capturing the student's attention and in getting the child to notice the letter. The word for the object begins with the particular sound of the letter portrayed on the picture. The letter is part of the object it represents to increase the association of the letter, its sound, and its appearance with the object. Point this out. The story ties it all together. Associating something ridiculous with something familiar is a proven method of increasing memory. Associating something known (the picture) with something new and unknown (the letter and its sound) helps the student remember the letter. For example, on the **short a** page, the words *alligator* and *apple* are not normally associated together, but an alligator hanging by his tail in an apple tree is unthinkable. The absurd story of the alligator in the apple tree incorporates visually and auditorily the letter and sound of short a by making the letter part of the picture. The more ridiculous something is, the easier it is to remember. An abstract idea is made more concrete through associating the letter to a picture.

Learn the story and characters well. Ask the student questions about the picture and the sound for the letter until it is easy to recall. For example, say, "Find the alligator. Do you see the capital A in the alligator's mouth and on his tail? Find the apple. Do you see the lower case a in the shape of the apple? Alligator and apple start with the short a sound." Make the short a sound several times, and have the student practice saying it correctly while looking in a mirror. Notice how the mouth moves while making this sound. For example, tell the student that the correct way to say the letter's sound is by saying only the first letter's sound in the words *alligator* or *apple*.

Spend plenty of time looking at the letter and noticing the direction the letter in the object is facing, when direction of the letter is applicable. On a whiteboard, practice making the letter correctly together. After the student can make both the capital and lower case letters correctly, ask them what object, animal, or thing from the book can be made from that letter. This uses visual memory. If the student cannot remember what was in the book, show them again. Be interesting, dramatic, and fun when explaining the details of the picture and story. Remove the picture and see if they can now recall what they saw. Repeat and review as often as needed. Thoroughly learn one letter at a time. Allow the student to copy from you (step by step) as you write the letter and transform it into the book's picture. A crude representation of the picture is sufficient.

Each long vowel on the Long Vowel Student Page shows two long vowel girls saying their names with their mouths in the shape of that particular letter. The long vowel girls are also wearing necklaces with their names on the necklaces. Emphasize that these are LONG vowels, so the long vowel girls are LONG and tall and say their names.

VISUALIZATION AND AUDITORY PERCEPTION

To remember each letter, remind students to think about and visualize the story and picture. Visualization increases memory tremendously. The letters are easy to visualize due to the fact that the letter is part of the object. Students can begin to interchange seeing just the letter and visualizing in their minds what animal, person, or object they remembered seeing in the book. A way to teach auditory perception is by making the short a sound and asking what word picture from the book would finish the word from that sound. They can also be helped when they see the letter anywhere now that they remember at least one word (the picture word) that begins with that letter. Visualization makes this possible. Train the students to close their eyes and see in their mind's eye what part of the picture the letter is representing. Teach your students to say the name of the picture, but only make the first letter's sound. This will correctly make the phonetic sound in isolation. The letters almost come to life and take on a personality in this book, which greatly enhances memory, association, visualization, and auditory memory for the students. Using the pictures in the book exclusively at first will help students know sounds on an automatic level. By knowing these fundamentals well without hesitation, reading becomes better.

Practice making the sound for a letter and ask what letter or story it matches. This will train the student's auditory perception. Use the picture in the book if needed and then conceal the picture. If a child is having trouble remembering what sound or picture goes with the letter, start to read, sing, or repeat the story, but omit the words that start with this letter. Let the student fill in the missing words. Drill and practice to fine tune auditory perception.

Check often to see if the child understands. Present concepts in ways the child can learn best. Go back frequently and let the child tell you in his own words what he understands to check for long-term memory recall.

Vowels and consonants will be taught in a similar manner, so follow the plan for each letter as given earlier. Anything known well could be skipped, but be sure the student's knowledge is solid. The severity of any learning disability or such problem will determine when to move on to a new letter and what needs to be skipped. Individualize this teaching to fit the needs of each student. Rely on the maturity, readiness, and age of students before teaching exceptions to the rules. Add the rules and the exceptions to the rules as deemed appropriate or necessary. Present several examples to go along with the rules and exceptions.

KINESTHETIC

Toward the bottom of each Student Page is a diagram showing the correct way to form the letters using numbers and arrows to direct each stroke of the pencil to follow strokes in numerical order. On the bottom of the Student Page is an alphabet strip of capital letters and underneath it is another alphabet strip of lower case letters. Underlined on both alphabet strips is the letter for that page to show where that letter comes in the alphabet.

For students who need additional help, practice writing the letter in the air using a stiff arm. Write the letter in sand, on the chalkboard, or on paper using various writing utensils. Use clay to form the letter. These kinesthetic approaches use movement to place the letters in memory. Placement of the mouth, lips, and tongue are noticed and felt to make students aware of how their mouths move when making the correct phonetic sounds.

On the Student Page students could finger trace letters for additional learning activities. Learn only one letter well at a time before moving on to another letter. Review often.

CONSONANTS

When working on consonant sounds, do not exaggerate the sound because when a consonant sound is exaggerated, it seems that a vowel sound has been added to it. Keep it a pure sound, shorten it and do not drag out the sound by adding an (uh) or an (ee) sound to the end of the consonant sound. Do not drop your jaw when making the consonant sound or you are exaggerating the isolated consonant sound. Practice making the consonant sounds until you can make them correctly. Make only the consonant sound and stop.

For reversals or flipping of letters: b, d, p, and q use the techniques in the book. Also show the student an alphabet strip to demonstrate that b comes before d, and p comes before q in the alphabet. Both you and the student are facing the alphabet strip. Discuss how when reading we go from left to right. On our left hand we can hold up our thumb to resemble the lower case b (see the book illustration). This principle holds true for d, p, and q also as explained in detail in the book. Go over this until they fully understand it. Make sure that you and the student are facing the same direction.

Emphasize that we read from left to right. b is on our left hand, and d is on our right hand. p is on our left hand and q is on our right hand. b comes before d in the alphabet, and p comes before q. Start to recite the alphabet and say, "A" (hold up left hand with the thumb up making the b) "B, C," (hold up right hand with the thumb up making the d) "D". Do this while both of you are facing an alphabet strip. The letters p and q should be done in the same way except the thumbs will be pointing down for these letters.

For students that confuse capital M and capital W, use the book's pictures to show that M has mountain peaks to ski down, and show that W has wheels on the bottom of the W wagon. The pictures help students figure out the direction of the letter by visualizing and associating the letter with the picture with which it begins. Each method in isolation is not nearly as effective as each method combined. Integrating the various learning modalities helps in learning anything more quickly. Using more of the senses helps retain more of the information to be learned.

Use these techniques, and you will begin to see students of any age succeed who have not been successful. It has worked many times for my students. They can now understand, remember, and use what they learned from this book.

DEDICATION

This book is dedicated to students with unconventional learning styles who learn and experience the world uniquely. I also dedicate this book to my own 2 wonderful children.

To Teachers and Parents: By using memory training techniques, multi-sensory approaches, making learning fun and interesting; you are changing the student/s lives in a positive way by making learning meaningful and memorable.

short Ă ă
vowel

Look in a mirror when you say ă to see how your mouth looks. Pay attention to how your tongue and lips move when making this sound.

For different name from sound vowels (or short vowels), the tongue goes down. When the tongue goes down, it's a short vowel sound.

Your mouth opens big like you are going to take a bite out of an apple.

Ă ă

In **short a** words there is usually just one vowel (the **a**) per syllable.

cat
_a_

On the student page:

- Emphasize that the letter looks like the object it represents.
- Find the capital A on the alligator's tail and mouth. Find the lower case a on the apples in the tree. Find the short a words alligator and apple in the story. .
- Practice tracing the letter correctly using the correct strokes. .
- Use large, stiff, arm strokes to draw the letter in the air.

Short Ă ă
vowel

A green *alligator* hung upside down by his tail to reach a red <u>apple</u> on a tree. A branch got stuck in his mouth.

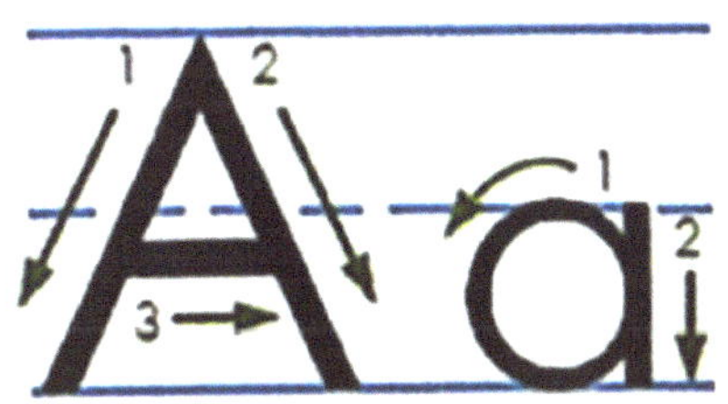

Capital A lower case a

<u>A</u> B C D E F G H I J K L M N O P Q R S T U V W X Y Z
<u>a</u> b c d e f g h i j k l m n o p q r s t u v w x y z

long Ā ā
vowel

For same name and sound vowels (long vowels), the tongue goes up. When the tongue goes up, it's a long vowel sound.

In long a words, there are usually two vowels per syllable. A comes first and says her name while the second vowel is quiet.

cake
_a_e

Tail
_ai_

Day
_ay

On the student page:

- Emphasize that the letter looks like the object it represents. Find the capital A on the apron and find the lower case a on the acorn in the picture.
- Practice tracing the letter correctly using correct strokes.
- Use large stiff arm strokes tracing the letter in the air.

long Ā ā
vowel

<u>a</u>corn <u>A</u>pron

<u>A</u>my wore <u>a</u> white <u>a</u>pron with pockets to gather <u>a</u>corns.

<u>A</u>my is <u>a</u> good helper.

The word a sounds like the name of this letter and like the sound the long <u>a</u> makes. Find the word <u>a</u> in the story.

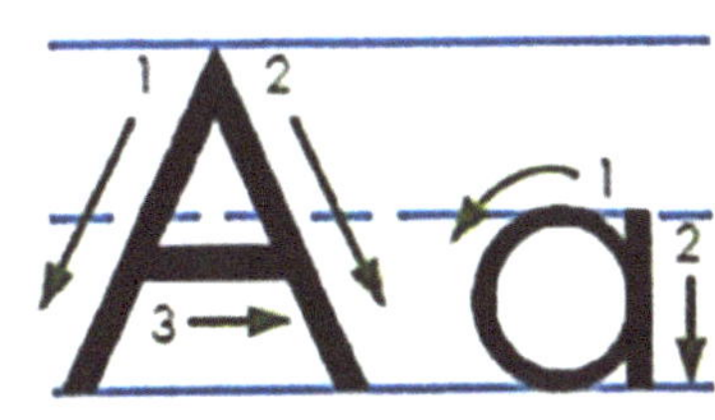

Capital A lower case a

Long A a says her name (Āā).

<u>A</u> B C D E F G H I J K L M N O P Q R S T U V W X Y Z
<u>a</u> b c d e f g h i j k l m n o p q r s t u v w x y z

B b
consonant

Look in a mirror when you say the b sound to see how your mouth looks. Pay attention to how your tongue and lips move when making this sound.

This is a loud or (voiced) sound. Use the front of your mouth or lips to make this sound. Don't put a vowel sound after the b. Make only the Bb sound and stop.

(On the student page emphasize that the letter looks like the object it represents.) .

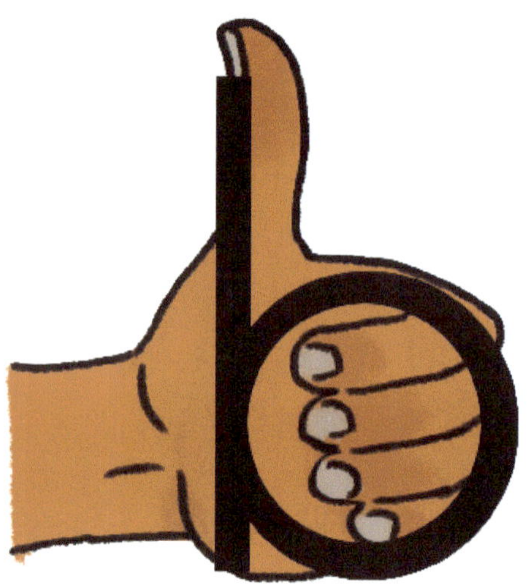

The left hand making a fist, with your thumb up, looks like the lower case b.

(On the student page, practice tracing the letter correctly using the correct strokes. Use large stiff arm strokes tracing the letter in the air, too.)
Find the capital B on the bee and butterfly picture.
Find the lower case b in the shape of the bat and ball.

B b
consonant

A <u>bee</u> landed on my <u>b</u>at and <u>b</u>all. I wish it could <u>be</u> a <u>b</u>utterfly.

<u>Bee</u>   <u>b</u>at <u>b</u>all   <u>B</u>utterfly

The <u>b</u>at comes first and next comes the <u>b</u>all.

Find the word <u>bee</u> and <u>be</u> in the story. The word <u>bee</u> is also the name of this letter.

Take the top off the capital B to make the lower case b.

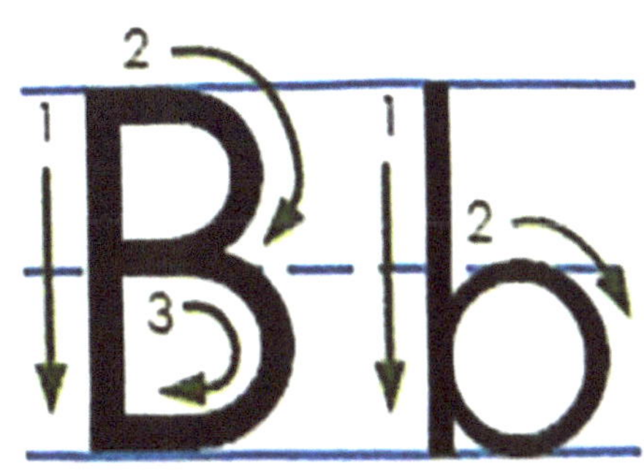

Capital B lower case b

The left hand making a fist, with your thumb up, looks like the lower case b.

A <u>B</u> C D E F G H I J K L M N O P Q R S T U V W X Y Z
a <u>b</u> c d e f g h i j k l m n o p q r s t u v w x y z

C c
consonant

When <u>Cc</u> borrows the <u>Kk</u> sound, it is a quiet sound. This sound is made towards the back of the throat. Find the <u>Kk</u> sound in this book and study it.

When <u>Cc</u> borrows the <u>Ss</u> sound, it is a quiet sound. It sounds like air coming from a tire. Find the Ss sound in this book and study it.

Look in a mirror when you say either one of the sounds for <u>Cc</u> to see how your mouth looks. Pay attention to how your tongue and lips move when making this sound.

Do not put a vowel sound after either one of the two sounds of <u>Cc</u>.

Find the c pictures on page 17. Find the c's on the eyes. Notice the c on the pictures of the cow and cat that sound like the letter k. Notice the ¢ on the pictures of the cent and city that sound like the letter s.

Remember to make learning fun.

Cc
consonant

Letter <u>C</u>c did not have its own sound.

All <u>C</u>c could do was <u>see</u> until he borrowed the sounds from <u>K</u>k and <u>S</u>s.

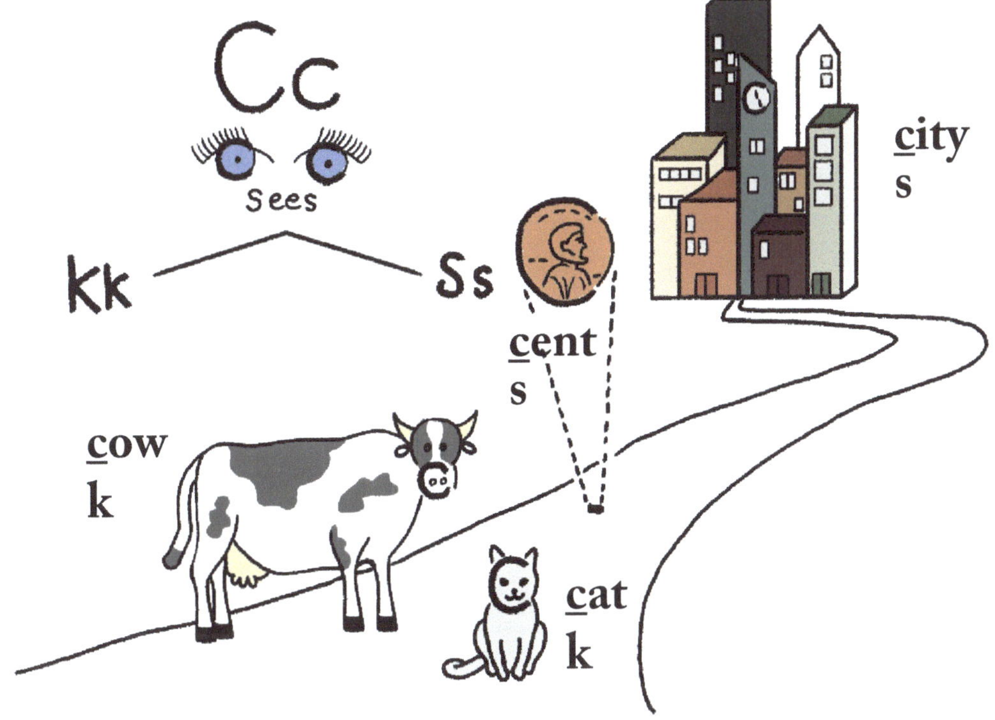

A <u>c</u>at and a <u>c</u>ow went to the <u>c</u>ity to spend one <u>c</u>ent and <u>see</u> everything.
Find the word <u>see</u> in the story.

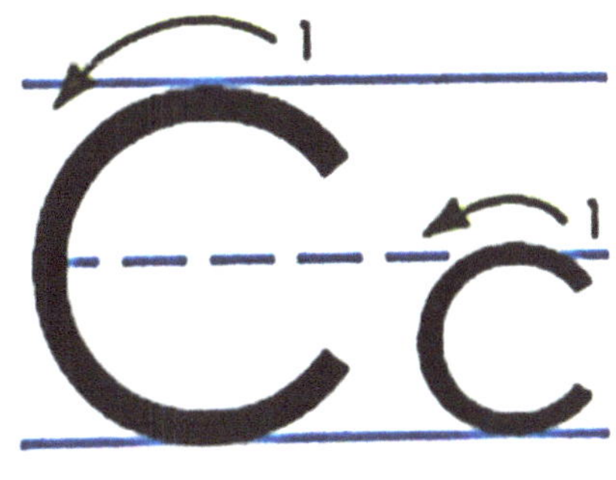

Capital C   **lower case c**

A B <u>C</u> D E F G H I J K L M N O P Q R S T U V W X Y Z
a b <u>c</u> d e f g h i j k l m n o p q r s t u v w x y z

D d
consonant

Look in a mirror when you say the d sound to see how your mouth looks. Pay attention to how your tongue and lips move when making this sound. Notice whether you use the front, middle, or back of your mouth while making this sound.

This is a loud or (voiced) sound. The middle of your mouth is used to make the <u>Dd</u> sound. Don't put a vowel sound after the <u>d</u>. Make only the <u>Dd</u> sound and stop. Put your hand on your throat to feel the vibration when saying the d sound.

(On the student page, emphasize that the letter looks like the object it represents.)

On page 19 find the capital D on the duck picture. On page 19 find the lower case d on the doorknob and door picture.

The right hand making a fist, with the thumb up, looks like the lower case <u>d</u>.

d

(On the student page, practice tracing the letter correctly using the correct strokes. Use large stiff arm strokes tracing the letter in the air, too.)

D d
consonant

Duck

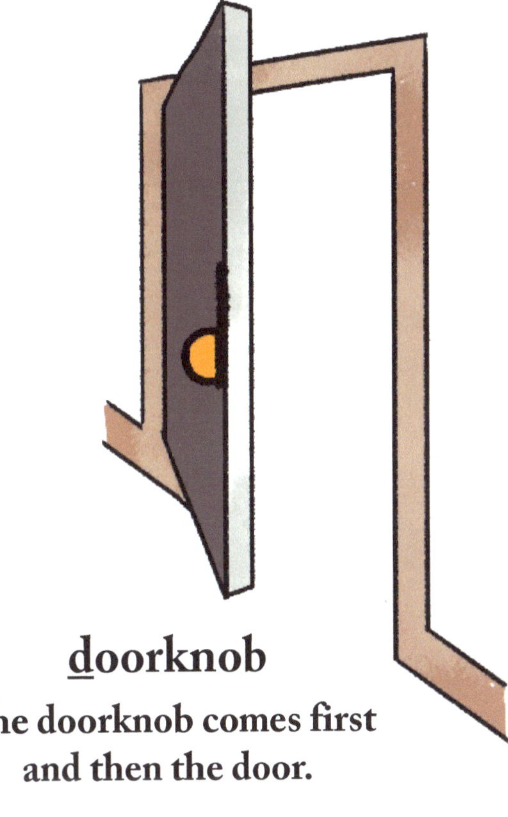

doorknob

**The doorknob comes first
and then the door.**

Dee Dee the duck turned the doorknob and opened the door.

The name <u>Dee</u> <u>Dee</u> sounds like the name of this letter. Find the word <u>Dee</u> in the story.

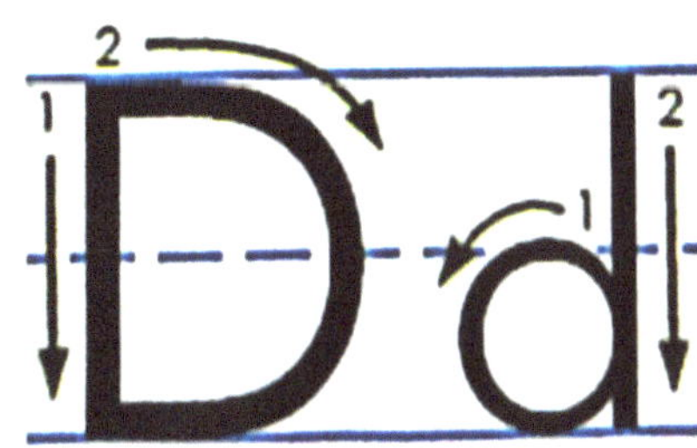

Capital D lower case d

A B C <u>D</u> E F G H I J K L M N O P Q R S T U V W X Y Z
a b c <u>d</u> e f g h i j k l m n o p q r s t u v w x y z

TEACHER/PARENT PAGE
(DIFFERENT NAME FROM SOUND A)

short Ĕ ĕ
vowel

Look in a mirror when you say **ĕ** to see how your mouth looks. Pay attention to how your tongue and lips move when making this sound.

For different name from sound vowels or (short vowels), When the tongue goes down, it's a short vowel.

Your mouth smiles slightly when you say **ĕ** because thinking of elephants and decorated eggs make you happy.

Ĕĕ

In short e words there is usually just one vowel. (the e) per syllable.

Bed
_e_

exception:

bread
__ea_

On the student page:

- Emphasize that the letter looks like the object it represents .
- Practice tracing the letter correctly using the correct strokes.
- Use large stiff arm strokes tracing the letter in the air.

short Ĕ ĕ
vowel

Ĕlephant   **ĕgg**

A cute e̲lephant got a pretty decorated e̲gg. That made him happy.

Find the capital E̲ on the elephant picture. Find the lower case e̲ on the egg picture.

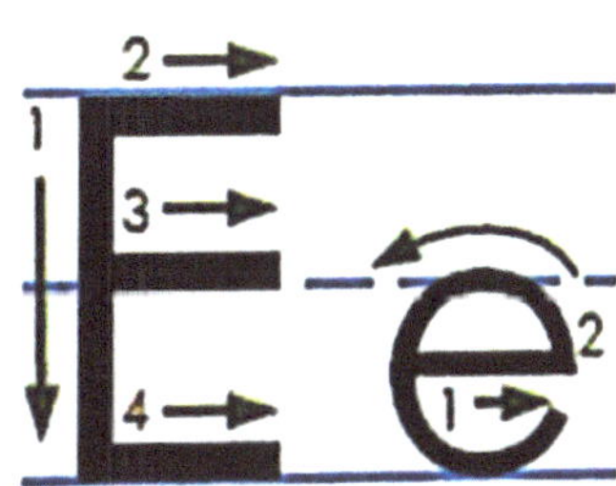

Capital E lower case e

A B C D E̲ F G H I J K L M N O P Q R S T U V W X Y Z
a b c d e̲ f g h i j k l m n o p q r s t u v w x y z

Long Ē ē
vowel

For same name and sound vowels (long vowels), the tongue goes up. When the tongue goes up, it's a long vowel sound.

In long e words there are usually 2 vowels per syllable. E comes first and says her name while the second vowel is quiet.

tr<u>ee</u>
__ee

<u>ea</u>t
ea_

exception: a short word with <u>e</u> as the last letter

h<u>e</u>
_e

Bunn<u>y</u>
_e

y at the end of some words says <u>Ee</u>

(On the student page, emphasize that the letter looks like the object it represents.)
(On the student page, practice tracing the letter correctly using the correct strokes. Use large stiff arm strokes tracing the letter in the air, too.)

Long Ē ē
vowel

ēagle

Ēasel

An eagle landed on Evie's easel. Evie was so scared she yelled, "E-e-e-e!"

Find the capital E on the Easel picture. Find the lower case e on the eagle and ear picture.

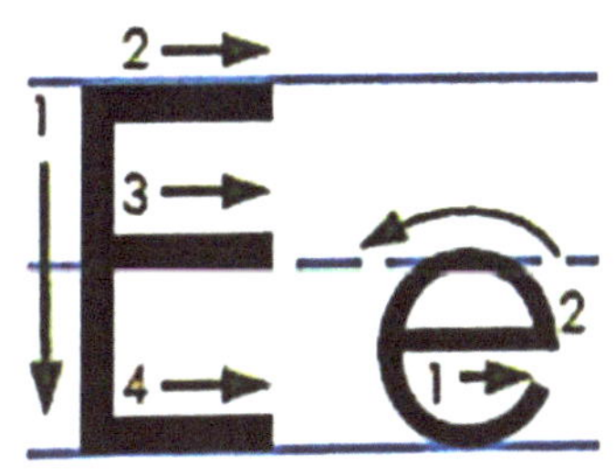

Capital E lower case e

Long Ee says her name (Ē ē)

A B C D E F G H I J K L M N O P Q R S T U V W X Y Z
a b c d e f g h i j k l m n o p q r s t u v w x y z

F f

consonant

Look in a mirror when you say the f sound to see how Your mouth looks. Pay attention to how your tongue and lips move when making this sound. Notice whether you use the front, middle, or back of your mouth while making this sound.

This is a quiet or (unvoiced) sound. Use the front of your mouth to make the sound for f. Place your front teeth over your bottom lip and make a blowing noise to sound like the f sound. An angry cat sounds like he is making the f sound. Don't put a vowel after the f. Make only the <u>Ff</u> sound and stop.

(On the student page, emphasize that the letter looks like the object it represents.)

(On the student page, practice tracing the letter correctly using the correct strokes.

Use large stiff arm strokes tracing the letter in the air, too.) Ph make the <u>Ff</u> sound as in <u>ph</u>one.

<u>ph</u>one

f

Find the capital <u>F</u> on the fish pictures. Find the lowercase <u>f</u> on the fish hook and fish picture.

F f
consonant

fish hook

F̲ish

The f̲ish tried to eat the worm from the upside down fish hook.
Emphasize that the letter looks like the object it represents.
An F̲ on a school paper means you failed.

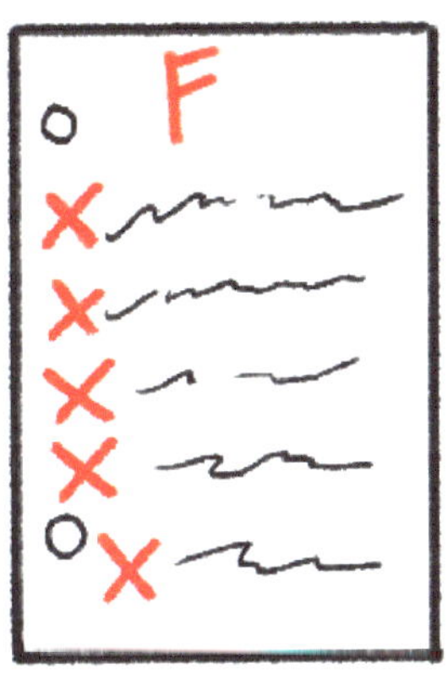

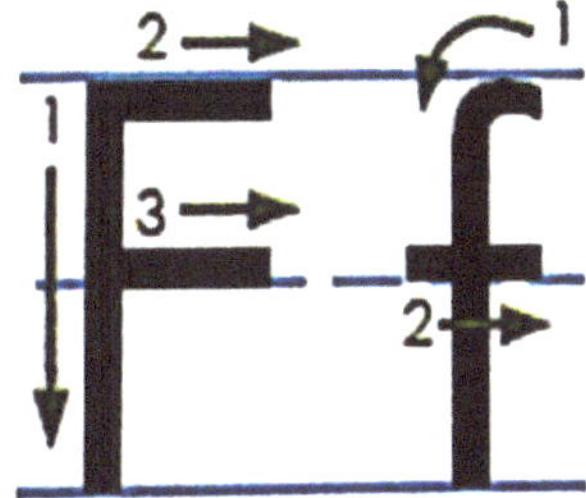

Capital F   lower case f

A B C D E F̲ G H I J K L M N O P Q R S T U V W X Y Z
a b c d e f̲ g h i j k l m n o p q r s t u v w x y z

G g
consonant

Look in a mirror when you say g sound to see how your mouth looks. Pay attention to how your tongue and lips move when making this sound. Notice whether you use the front, ,iddle, or back of your mouth while making this sound. Put your hand on your throat to feel the vibration when saying the g sound.

This is a loud or (voiced) sound. Make the sound for g deep in your throat. Remember this rhyme:

Deep in the throat
Say g-g goat.

Don't put a vowel sound after the g. Make only the Gg sound and stop.

On the student page:
- Emphasize that the letter looks like the object it represents.
- Find the capital G on the goat picture. Find the lower case g on the guitar picture.
- Practice tracing the letter correctly using the correct strokes.
- Use large stiff arm strokes tracing the letter in the air.

Name the 5 vowels (a, e, i, o, u) and find the vowels on the alphabet strip.

Name the consonants b, c, d, f, g, h, j, k, l, m, n, p, q, r, s, t, v, w, x, y, z and find them on the alphabet strip.

G g
consonant

Goat　　　　**g**uitar

Gee Gee the goat heard the guitar and tried to eat it. I said, "Gee!" "Stop that goat!"

The name Gee Gee sounds like the name of this letter.

Find the word Gee in the story.

Capital G　　lower case g

A B C D E F G H I J K L M N O P Q R S T U V W X Y Z
a b c d e f g h i j k l m n o p q r s t u v w x y z

H h
consonant

Look in a mirror when you say the h sound to see how your mouth looks. Pay attention to how your tongue and lips move when making this sound. Notice whether you use the front, middle, or back of your mouth while making this sound.

This is a quiet or (unvoiced) sound that is made in the back of your throat. When you've been running and start breathing hard, you are making the h sound h-h-h. Leave off any vowel sounds from the end of h to get the correct sound for h.

On the student page:

- Emphasize that the Jetter looks like the object it represents.
- Find the capital H on the house picture and the sign. Find the lower case h on the hat picture and the sound coming from Hudson's mouth as he runs.
- Practice tracing the letter correctly using the correct strokes.
- Use large stiff arm strokes tracing the letter in the air.

Reminder for teachers:

Count syllables by sounded vowels (the number of divisions, intervals, or accents stressed per vocalized word with claps or beats.) Use a dictionary when needed

eat = 1 syllable word, Hudson = 2 syllable word, butterfly = 3 syllable word

H h
consonant

<u>H</u>ouse Ave. <u>H</u>   **<u>h</u>at**

<u>H</u>udson was running down Ave. <u>H</u> to <u>h</u>is <u>h</u>ouse while wearing <u>h</u>is <u>h</u>at. <u>H</u>e was so <u>h</u>ot and tired that <u>h</u>e made the <u>h</u> sound. h-h-h

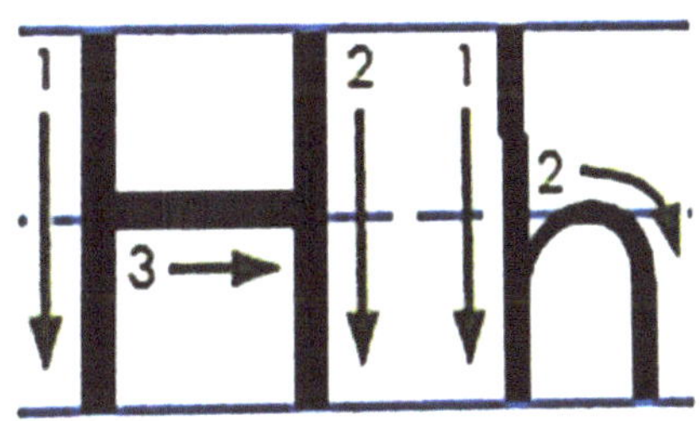

Capital H   lower case h

A B C D E F G <u>H</u> I J K L M N O P Q R S T U V W X Y Z
a b c d e f g <u>h</u> i j k l m n o p q r s t u v w x y z

TEACHER/PARENT PAGE
(DIFFERENT NAME FROM SOUND I)

short Ĭ ĭ
vowel

Look in a mirror when you say ĭ to see how your mouth looks. Pay attention to how your tongue and lips move when making this sound.

For different name from sound vowels or (short vowels), the tongue goes down. When the tongue goes down, it's a short vowel sound.

Your mouth opens only a little when you make the short i sound. Think of the little door of the igloo when you make this sound and only open your mouth a little for ĭ.

Ĭĭ

In short i words there is usually just one vowel (the i) per syllable.

Fish
_i__

On the student page:
- Emphasize that the letter looks like the object it represents.
- Find the capital I on the Inuit and the lower case i on the igloo picture
- Practice tracing the letter correctly using the correct strokes.
- Use large stiff arm strokes tracing the letter in the air.

short Ĭ ĭ
vowel

Ĭnuit   **ĭgloo**

An Ĭnuit climbed ĭnto the little door of an ĭgloo. The Ĭnuit got a little shut eye when he fell asleep ĭnside the ĭgloo until I woke him.

The words (I) and (eye) sound like the name of this letter. Find the words *I* and *eye* in the story.

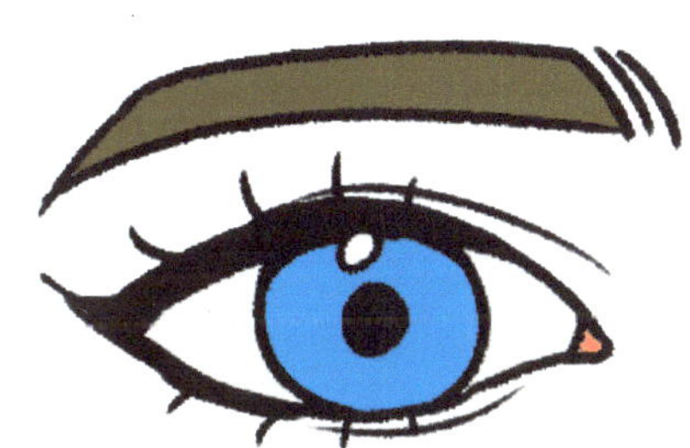

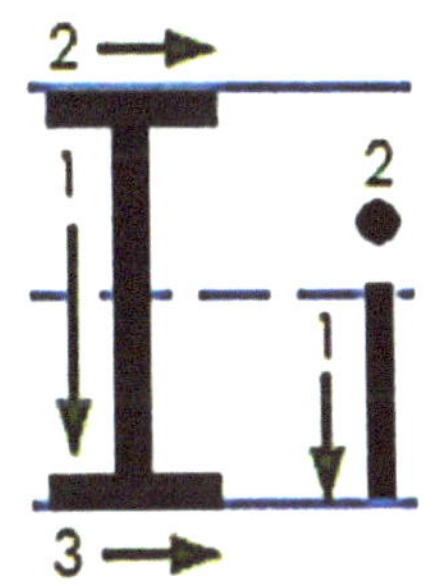

**eye sounds
like the name of letter Ii**

A B C D E F G H I J K L M N O P Q R S T U V W X Y Z
a b c d e f g h i j k l m n o p q r s t u v w x y z

TEACHER/PARENT PAGE (SAME NAME AND SOUND I)

long Ī ī
vowel

For same name and sound vowels (long vowels), the tongue goes up. When the tongue goes up, it's a long vowel sound.

In long i words there is usually two vowels per syllable. I comes first and says her name while the second vowel is quiet.

exceptions:

5

five
_i_e

night
igh
igh say I

fly
__y
_y says i when y is at the
end of some words

On the student page:

- Emphasize that the letter looks like the object it represents
- Find the capital I on the iron and the lower case i on the ice cream picture.
- Practice tracing the letter correctly using the correct strokes.
- Use large stiff arm strokes tracing the letter in the air.

long Ī ī
vowel

Īron   **īce cream**   **eye**

I set my hot iron too close to my ice cream and it began to melt. I saw it from the corner of my eye and I moved it.

The words (I) and (eye) sound like the Name and sound of this letter.

Find them in the story.

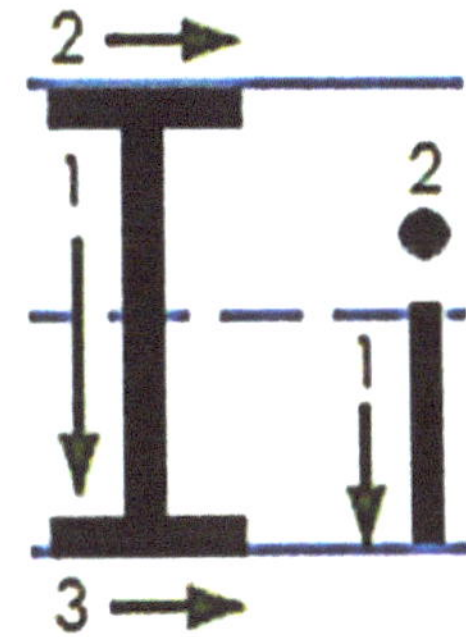

Capital I lower case i

Long I i says her name (Ī ī).

A B C D E F G H I J K L M N O P Q R S T U V W X Y Z
a b c d e f g h i j k l m n o p q r s t u v w x y z

Jj
consonant

Look in a mirror when you say the j sound to see how your mouth looks. Pay attention to how your tongue and lips move when making this sound. Notice whether you use the front, middle, or back of your mouth while making this sound.

(On the student page, emphasize that the letter looks like the object it represents.)

Find capital J on the Jar picture. Find lower case j on the jack-o-lantern picture.

(On the student page, practice tracing the letter correctly using the correct strokes. Use large stiff arm strokes tracing the letter in the air, too.)

Sing the alphabet song.

Necessary repetitions can be enhanced with singing.

Clap when you sing the vowels a, e, i, o, u in the alphabet song.

J j
consonant

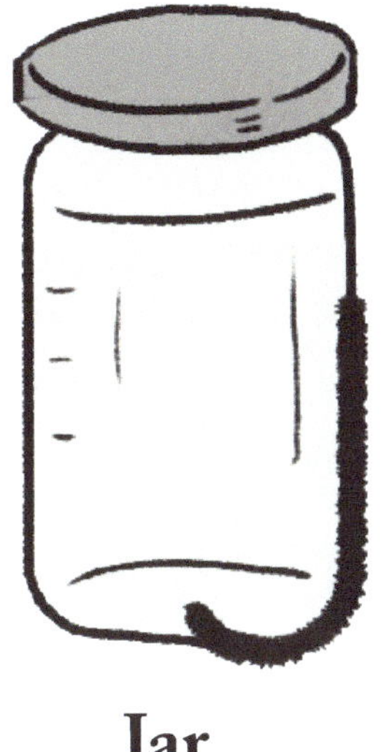

Jar

jack-o-lantern

A boy named <u>Jay</u> set a jar of candy and a jack-o-lantern on his window sill at Halloween.

The boy's name, <u>Jay</u>, sounds like the name of this letter. Find the name <u>Jay</u> in the story.

In some words, the <u>g</u> borrows the j sound as in <u>g</u>iant.
(j)

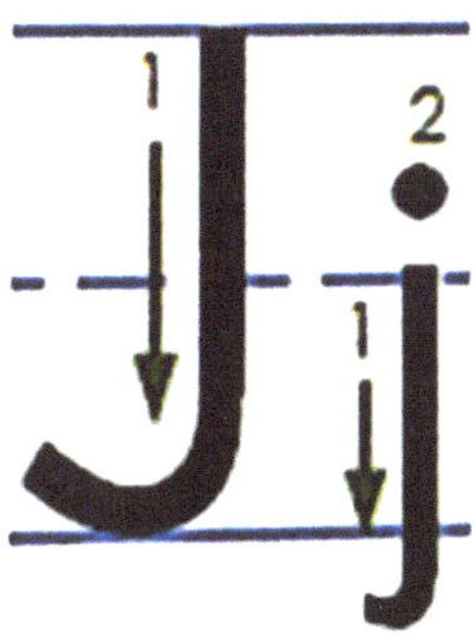

Capital J lower case j

A B C D E F G H I <u>J</u> K L M N O P Q R S T U V W X Y Z
a b c d e f g h i <u>j</u> k l m n o p q r s t u v w x y z

K k
consonant

Look in a mirror when you say the k sound to see how your mouth looks. Pay attention to how your tongue and lips move when making this sound. Notice whether you use the front, middle, or back of your mouth while making this sound.

<u>K</u> is a quiet or (unvoiced) sound that is made near the back of your throat. The mouth is open when the <u>k</u> sound is made. Practice making the <u>k</u> sound without adding any vowel sound at the end of the <u>k</u> sound. -ck and c borrow <u>k</u>'s sound sometimes.

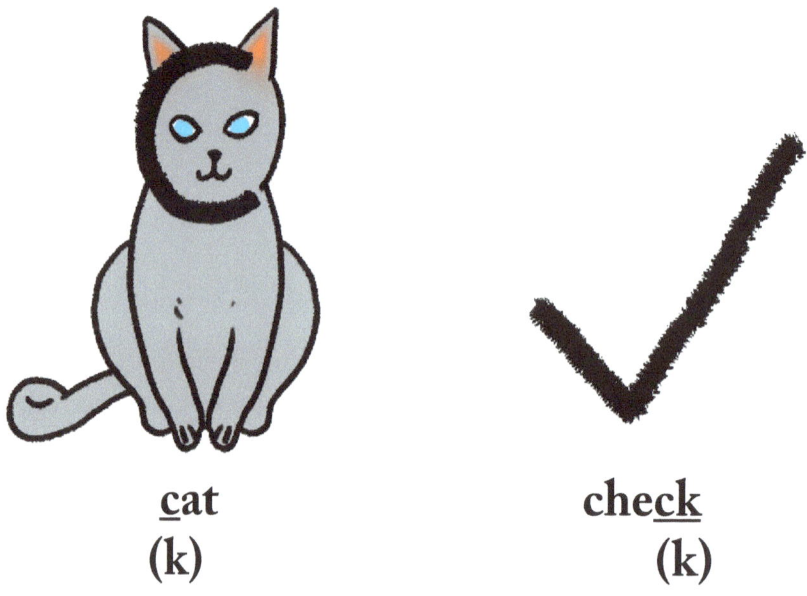

<u>c</u>at
(k)

che<u>ck</u>
(k)

ck sounds like only one letter, ck sounds like the letter <u>k</u>.

On the student page:
- Emphasize that the letter looks like the object it represents.
- Find the capital K's on the crown and the lower case <u>k</u> on the kite picture.
- Practice tracing the letter correctly using the correct strokes.
- Use large stiff arm strokes tracing the letter in the air.

K k
consonant

My friend, <u>K</u>ay, saw the <u>K</u>ing flying his new <u>k</u>ite.

The girl's name, <u>K</u>ay, sounds like the name of this letter. Find the word <u>Kay</u> in the story.

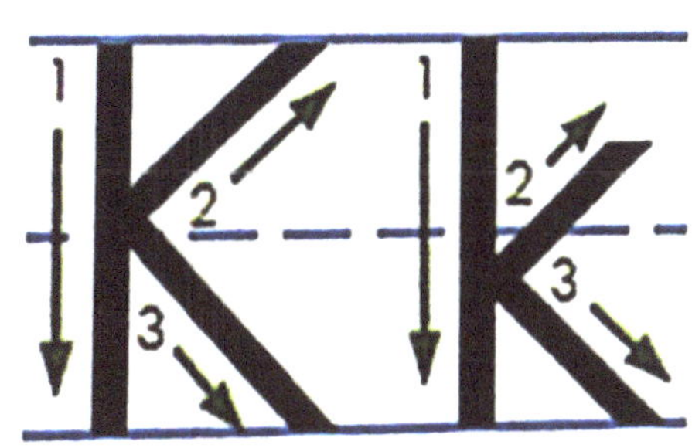

Capital K lower case k

A B C D E F G H I J <u>K</u> L M N O P Q R S T U V W X Y Z
a b c d e f g h i j <u>k</u> l m n o p q r s t u v w x y z

L l
consonant

Look in a mirror when you say the L sound see how your mouth looks. Pay attention to how your tongue and lips move when making this sound. Notice whether you use the front, middle, or back of your mouth while making this sound.

Put the tip of your tongue behind your teeth, pointing towards the roof of your mouth to make the L sound. The mouth is open when saying the L sound. To make the L sound correctly, do not add a vowel sound to the end of the L sound. The tongue curls up when saying L.

On the student page:

- Emphasize that the letter looks like the object it represents.
- Find the capital L on the Lollipop picture. Find the lower case l on the lollipop stick picture.
- Practice tracing the letter correctly using the correct strokes.
- Use large stiff arm strokes tracing the letter in the air.

Reminder: Encourage and praise efforts.

L l
consonant

Large
lollipop

Lou Ella licked a large lemon-flavored lollipop.

A nickname for Ella is El or L. This sounds like the name of the letter L.

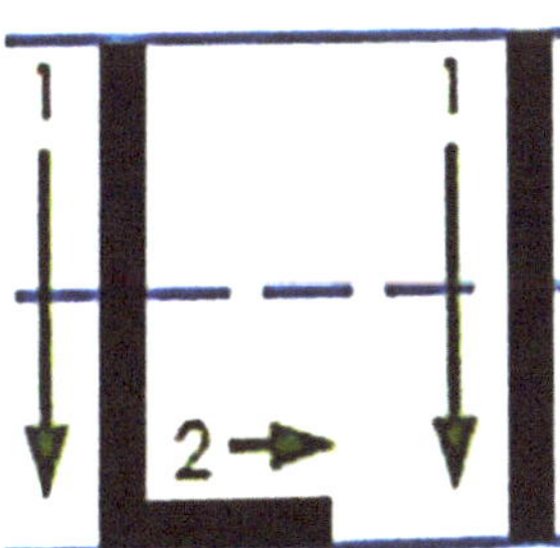

capital L   lower case l

A B C D E F G H I J K L M N O P Q R S T U V W X Y Z

a b c d e f g h i j k l m n o p q r s t u v w x y z

M m
consonant

Look in a mirror when you say the m sound to see how your mouth looks. Pay attention to how your tongue and lips move when making this sound. Notice whether you use the front, middle, or back of your mouth while making this sound.

This is a humming sound. Put your lips together and hum when you make the <u>m</u> sound. You eat m & m candy with your mouth, and you hum with your mouth while making the <u>m</u> sound.

On the student page:

- Emphasize that the letter looks like the object it represents.
- Find the capital M on the big mountain with sharp peaks picture. Find the lower case m on the little mountain picture.
- Practice tracing the letter correctly using the correct strokes.
- Use large stiff arm strokes tracing the letter in the air.

**Don't put a vowel sound after the m sound.
Use the front of your mouth to make the m sound.**

M m
consonant

Big <u>M</u>ountain　　　**little <u>m</u>ountain**　　　**<u>m</u>&<u>m</u> candy**

Emma and <u>M</u>ike skied down the big <u>m</u>ountain and the little <u>m</u>ountain. <u>M</u>ike yelled to <u>Em</u>, "When we finish skiing, let's eat some <u>m</u> & <u>m</u>'s." <u>Em</u> said, "<u>M</u>-<u>m</u>-<u>m</u>-<u>m</u>!" She was rubbing her tummy and smiling.

Emma's nickname, <u>Em</u>, sounds like the name of this letter.

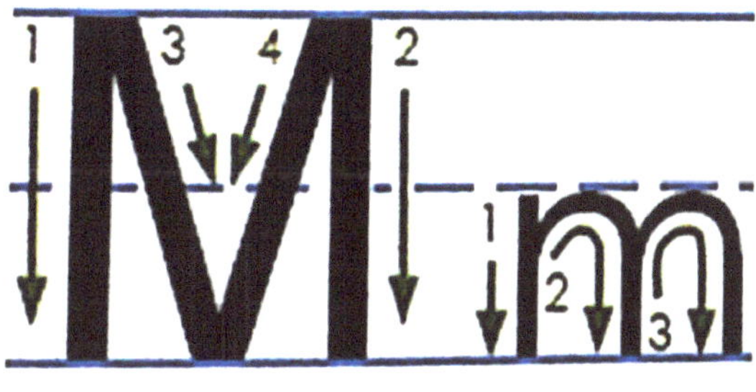

Capital M lower case m

A B C D E F G H I J K L <u>M</u> N O P Q R S T U V W X Y Z
a b c d e f g h i j k l <u>m</u> n o p q r s t u v w x y z

N n
consonant

Look in a mirror when you say the n sound to see how your mouth looks. Pay attention to how your tongue and lips move when making this sound. Notice whether you use the front, middle, or back of your mouth while making this sound.

Use the middle of your mouth to make the n sound. Put your relaxed tongue to the top of your mouth and hum using a nasal sound. The n sound comes through your <u>nose</u>. <u>N</u> is a humming sound. After you've said the n sound, stop. Practice making just the <u>Nn</u> sound without adding a vowel sound to the end of the <u>n</u>.

On the student page:

- Emphasize that the letter looks like the object it represents.
- Find the capital N on Ned's Nose picture. Find the lower case n on the nurse's nose picture.
- Practice tracing the letter correctly using the correct strokes.
- Use large stiff arm strokes tracing the letter in the air.

Practice writing correctly the letters that were hard.

Practice making letters with Play Doh.

N n
consonant

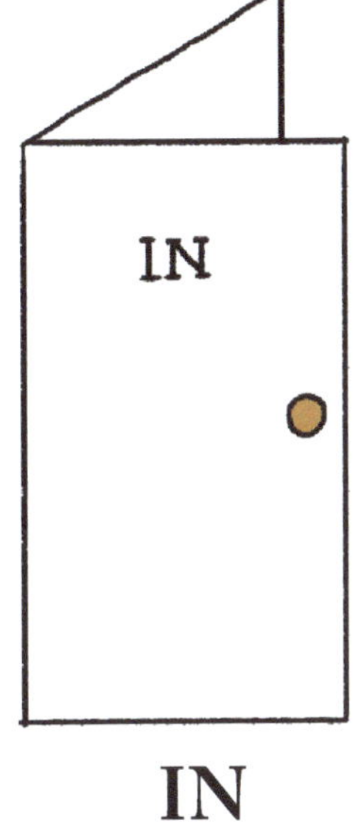

IN

Ned
Nose

nurse's
nose

Ned bumped his nose when he came in the door. Ned had the nurse check his nose.

The word in sounds like the letter Nn. Find the word in in the story.

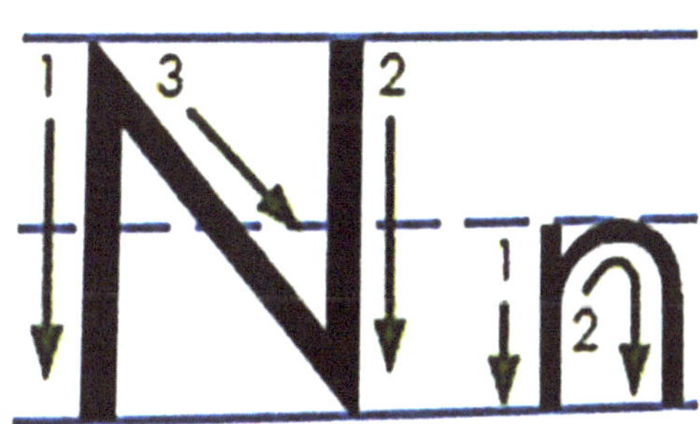

Capital N   lower case n

A B C D E F G H I J K L M N O P Q R S T U V W X Y Z
a b c d e f g h i j k l m n o p q r s t u v w x y z

short Ŏ ŏ vowel

Look in a mirror when you say ŏ to see how your mouth looks. Pay attention to how your tongue and lips move when making this sound.

For different name from sound vowels or (short vowels), the tongue goes down. When the tongue goes down, it's a short vowel sound.

Your mouth opens in an O shape when saying ŏ. You could pop an olive in your mouth when saying ŏ. We sometimes say "ah" (ŏ) when we are surprised. The doctor tells you to say "ah" when he wants to look at your throat.

Ŏŏ

In short <u>o</u> words, there is usually just one vowel (the o) per syllable.

top
_o_

On the student page:
- Emphasize that the letter looks like the object it represents.
- Practice tracing the letter correctly using the correct strokes .
- Use large stiff arm strokes tracing the letter in the air.
- Find the capital O on the Ox and the lower case o's on the octopus.

short Ŏ ŏ vowel

Ŏx   ŏctopus

An o̲x riding o̲n a boat fell into the ocean.

An o̲ctopus saw him and helped the o̲x get back into the boat. The o̲x said, "A̲h, you are so nice, octopus!"

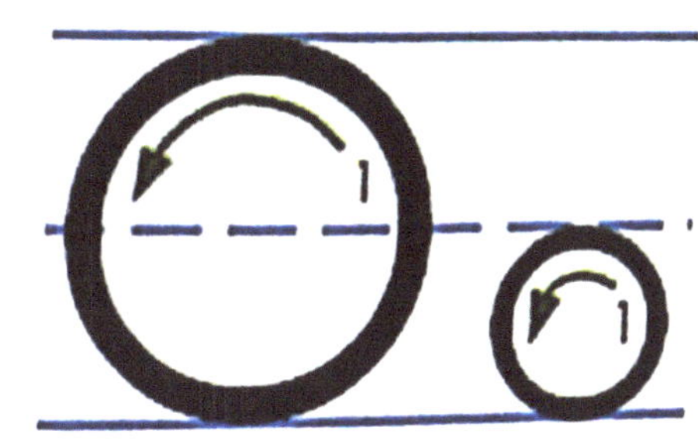

Capital O   lower case o

A B C D E F G H I J K L M N O̲ P Q R S T U V W X Y Z
a b c d e f g h i j k l m n o̲ p q r s t u v w x y z

TEACHER/PARENT PAGE
(SAME NAME AND SOUND O)

long Ō ō
vowel

For same name and sound vowels, (long vowels), the tongue goes up. When the tongue goes up, it's a long vowel sound.

In long o words there is usually two vowels per syllable. <u>O</u> comes first and says her name while the second vowel is quiet.

nose
_o_e

boat
_oa_

bow
_ow

exception: a short word with o as the last letter and o is the only vowel

go
_o

On the student page:
- Emphasize that the letter looks like the object it represents.
- Find capital O on the Ocean liner & lower case o on the overalls.
- Practice tracing the letter correctly using the correct strokes
- Use large stiff arm strokes tracing the letter in the air.

long Ō ō vowel

<u>O</u>cean
<u>o</u>cean liner

<u>o</u>veralls

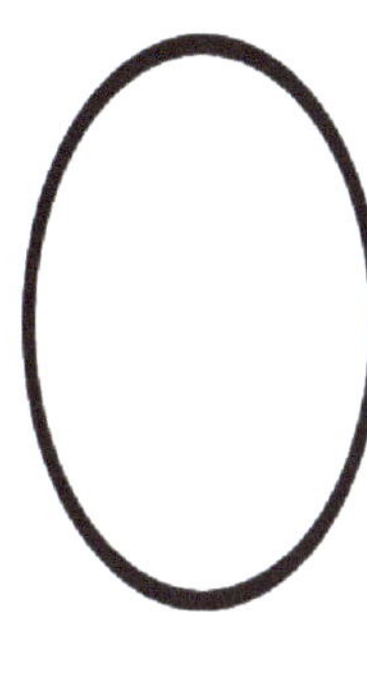

<u>o</u>val

A farmer on an ocean liner accidentally dropped his pair of <u>o</u>veralls, with the <u>o</u>val buttons, into the Pacific <u>O</u>cean. Long Oo saw it happen and said, "<u>Oh</u> no!"

The word <u>Oh</u> said when you are surprised, sounds like the name and sound of this letter. Find the word <u>Oh</u> in the story.

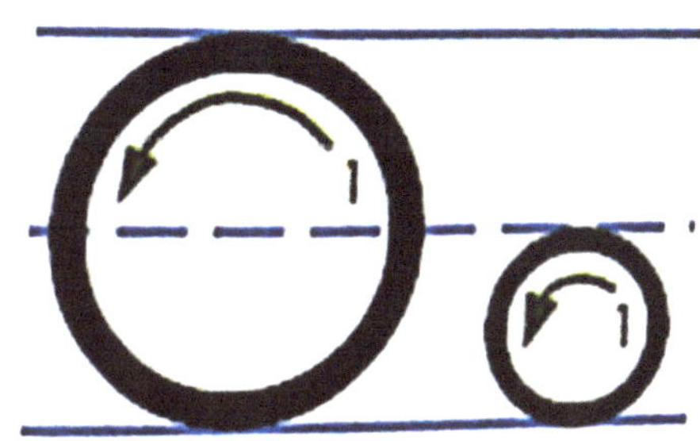

Capital O lower case o

Long Oo says her name (Ōō).

A B C D E F G H I J K L M N <u>O</u> P Q R S T U V W X Y Z
a b c d e f g h i j k l m n <u>o</u> p q r s t u v w x y z

P p
consonant

Look in a mirror when you say the p̲ sound to see how your mouth looks. Pay attention to how your tongue and lips move when making this sound. Notice whether you use the front, middle, or back of your mouth while making this sound.

This is a quiet or (unvoiced) sound. The front of your mouth is used to make the sound. Use the lips to make this p sound. Put the lips together and blow a small puff of air. Don't put a vowel sound after the p̲. Make only the P̲p̲ sound and stop.

On the student page:

- Emphasize that the letter looks like the object it represents.
- Find the capital P on the pig and lower case p's on the pizza.
- Practice tracing the letter correctly using the correct strokes.
- Use large stiff arm strokes tracing the letter in the air.

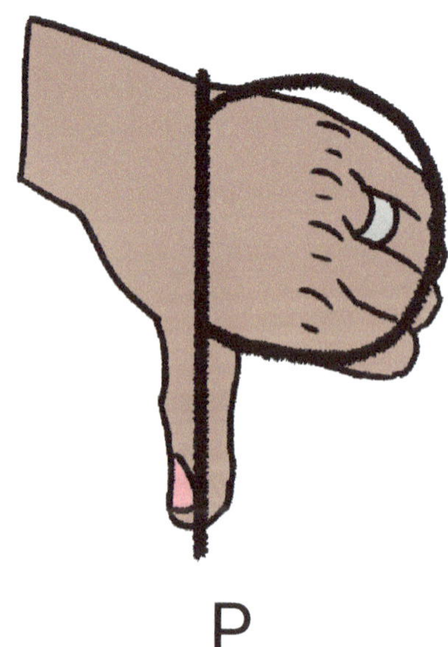

P

The left hand making a fist, with the thumb down, looks like the lower case p and the capital P.

P p
consonant

Pee Wee the pink pig

pepperoni pizza

Pee Wee the pink pig likes to eat pepperoni's in the shape of p's on his pizza. The first part of Pee Wee's name sounds like the name of this letter.

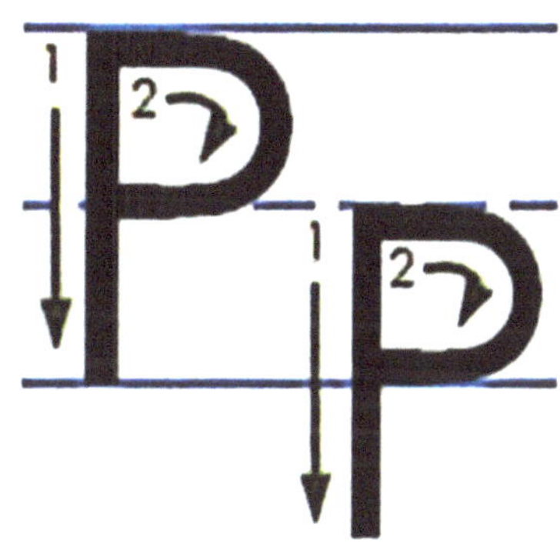

Capital P lower case p

A B C D E F G H I J K L M N O P Q R S T U V W X Y Z
a b c d e f g h i j k l m n o p q r s t u v w x y z

Q q
consonant

Look in a mirror when you say the q sound to see how your n"mouth looks. Pay attention to how your tongue and lips move when making this sound. Notice whether you use the front, middle, or back of your mouth while making this sound.

This is a loud or (voiced) sound. U usually comes after the q (Qu or qu). Q wants u to be by her. Q sounds like k and w put together (kw).

On the student page:

- Emphasize that the letter looks like the object it represents.
- Find the capital Q on the Queen's face shape, crown, necklace and quilt. Find the lower case q on the queen's face shape, crown, necklace, and quilt.
- Practice tracing the letter correctly using the correct strokes.
- Use large stiff arm strokes tracing the letter in the air.

The right hand making a fist, with the thumb pointing down, looks like the lower case q.

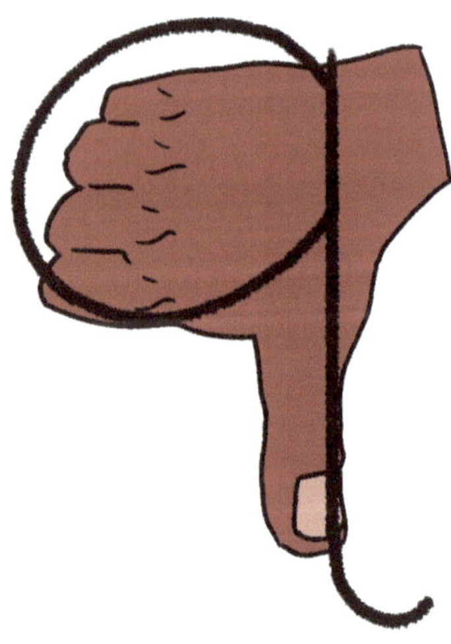

q

Q q
consonant

Queen

quilt

queen

After Queen Quincy finished dinner, she had a toothpick in her mouth. Her friend, the queen of Quebec, came over to bring Queen Quincy a new Qq pattern quilt for her queen-size bed. She lived on Ave. Q.

Capital Q lower case q

A B C D E F G H I J K L M N O P Q R S T U V W X Y Z
a b c d e f g h i j k l m n o p q r s t u v w x y z

R r
consonant

Look in a mirror when you say the r sound to see how your mouth looks. Pay attention to how your tongue and lips move when making this sound. Notice whether you use the front, middle, or back of your mouth while making this sound.

This is a loud sound. It sounds like a running motor. In order to make this sound correctly, do <u>not</u> make an <u>r</u> sound like an er sound. Start to say red and stop after making only the r sound. Do not put a vowel sound at the end of <u>r</u> either.

On the student page:

- Emphasize that the letter looks like the object it represents.
- Find capital R on the Rabbit picture. Find lower case r on the ring picture.
- Practice tracing the letter correctly using the correct strokes.
- Use large stiff arm strokes tracing the letter in the air.

Find all the consonant letters and write them down.

R r
consonant

ruby red ring

Rabbit

Robert Rabbit found a ruby red ring in the radish garden. "We are proud of you rabbit!", said the Ross family. The Ross family lost the red ring last week.

The word are sounds like the name of this letter. Find the word are in the story.

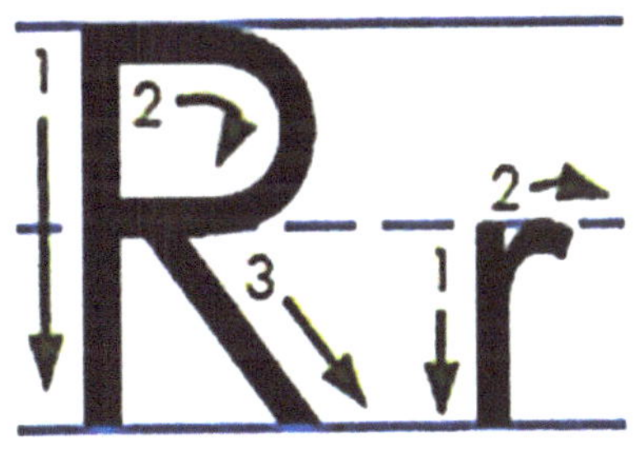

Capital R lower case r

A B C D E F G H I J K L M N O P Q R S T U V W X Y Z
a b c d e f g h i j k l m n o p q r s t u v w x y z

S s
consonant

Look in a mirror when you say the s sound to see how your mouth looks. Pay attention to how your tongue and lips move when making this sound. Notice whether you use the front, middle, or back of your mouth while making this sound.

<u>S</u> is a quiet or (unvoiced) sound. It sounds like air coming from a tire or the sound a rattlesnake makes. Don't put a vowel sound after the s sound. c borrows the <u>s</u> sound sometimes.

<u>c</u>ircus
(s)

<u>c</u>ity
(s)

On the student page:
- Emphasize that the letter looks like the object it represents.
- Find capital S on the Snake & lower case s on the seal.
- Practice tracing the letter correctly using the correct strokes.
- Use large stiff arm strokes tracing the letter in the air.

Sometimes s sounds like a z.

Example: i<u>s</u>
             (z)

S s
consonant

S̲am the s̲nake   **S̲id the s̲eal**

S̲am the s̲nake, liked to make the s̲ sound. S̲am's friend S̲id, the s̲eal, said, "Follow me to the circus."

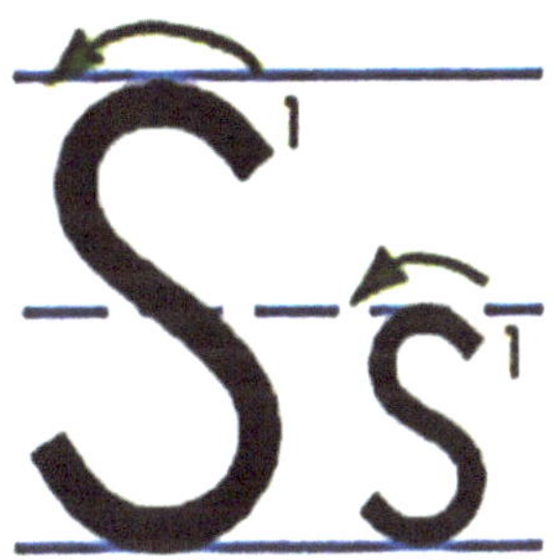

Capital S lower case s

A B C D E F G H I J K L M N O P Q R S̲ T U V W X Y Z
a b c d e f g h i j k l m n o p q r s̲ t u v w x y z

T t
consonant

Look in a mirror when you say the t sound to see how your mouth looks. Pay attention to how your tongue and lips move when making this sound. Notice whether you use the front, middle, or back of your mouth while making this sound.

T makes a quiet or (unvoiced) sound. The tongue quickly touches the roof of the mouth and then goes back down. Don't put a vowel sound after the t sound.

On the student page:

- Emphasize that the letter looks like the object it represents.
- Find capital T on the Table & TV and lower case t on the 2nd table.
- Practice tracing the letter correctly using the correct strokes.
- Use large stiff arm strokes tracing the letter in the air.

Reminder for teachers: Count syllables by sounded vowels (the number of divisions, intervals, or accents stressed per vocalized word with claps or beats.)

Use a dictionary when needed.

cat = 1 syllable word, ocean = 2 syllable word, lollipop = 3 syllable word

T t
consonant

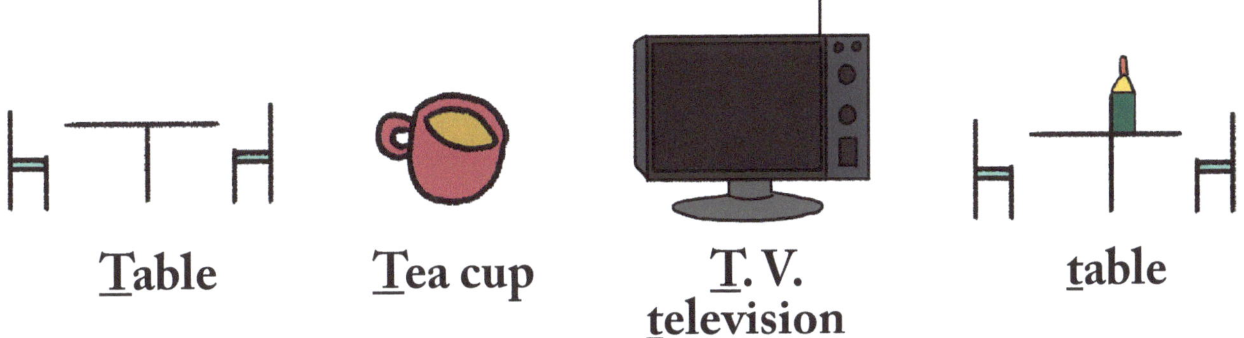

Table   Tea cup   T. V. television   table

Tim and Tiffany sat at the table drinking tea. They turned on the t. v. and watched a program starring Mr. T by candlelight.

The name of this letter sounds like the words tea, t.v., and Mr. T. Find these words in the story.

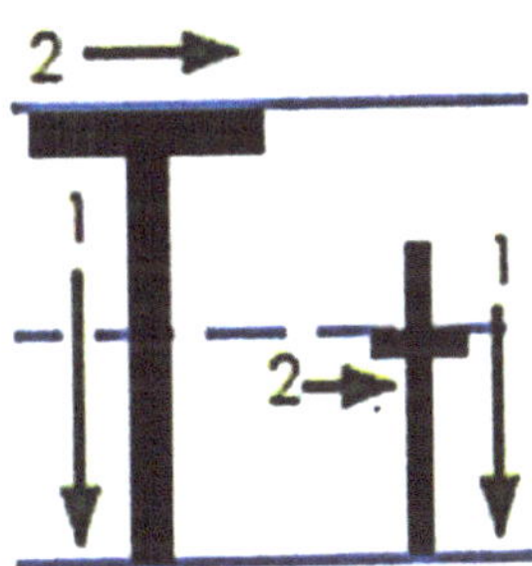

Capital T lower case t

A B C D E F G H I J K L M N O P Q R S T U V W X Y Z
a b c d e f g h i j k l m n o p q r s t u v w x y z

short Ŭ ŭ vowel

Look in a mirror when you say ŭ to see how your mouth looks. Pay attention to how your tongue and lips move when making this sound.

For different name from sound vowels or (short vowels), the tongue goes down. When the tongue goes down, it's a short vowel sound. Sometimes you say, "Uh" (Ŭ), when you are thinking.

Ŭŭ

In short <u>u</u> words there is usually just one vowel (the ŭ) per syllable.

Duck
_u__

On the student page:
- Emphasize that the letter looks like the object it represents.
- Find capital U on the 1st Umbrella & lower case u on the 2nd umbrella.
- Practice tracing the letter correctly using the correct strokes.
- Use large stiff arm dtrokes tracing the letter in the air.

short Ŭ ŭ
vowel

**Ŭpside down
Umbrella**

ŭmbrella

You can carry your umbrella upside down until it begins to rain. When the rain starts to fall, turn your umbrella upright to keep the rain off of you.

The word you sounds like the name of this letter. Find the word you in the story.

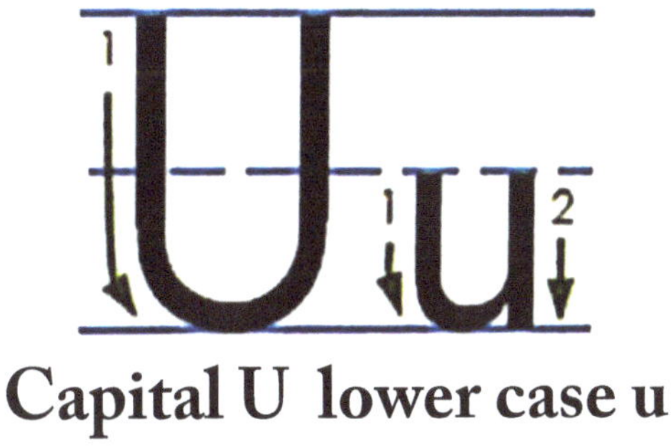

Capital U lower case u

A B C D E F G H I J K L M N O P Q R S T U V W X Y Z
a b c d e f g h i j k l m n o p q r s t u v w x y z

TEACHER/PARENT PAGE
(SAME NAME AND SOUND U)

long Ū ū
vowel

For same name and sound vowels (long vowels), the tongue goes up. When the tongue goes up, it's a long vowel sound.

In long u words there are usually two vowels per syllable. U comes first and says her name while the second vowel is quiet.

mule
_u_e

On the student page:
- Emphasize that the letter looks like the object it represents
- Find capital U on the Unicycle & lower case u on the unicorn.
- Practice tracing the letter correctly using the correct strokes.
- Use large stiff arm strokes tracing the letter in the air.

long Ū ū
vowel

Ūnicycle

ūnicorn

Did <u>you</u> see a <u>u</u>nicycle roll by the <u>u</u>nicom?

The word <u>you</u> sounds like the name of this letter and the name of the long <u>u</u> sound. Find the word <u>you</u> in the story.

Capital U lower case u

Long Uu says her name (Ūū).

A B C D E F G H I J K L M N O P Q R S T <u>U</u> V W X Y Z
a b c d e f g h i j k l m n o p q r s t <u>u</u> v w x y z

TEACHER/PARENT PAGE

V v
consonant

Look in a mirror when you say the v sound to see how your mouth looks. Pay attention to how your tongue and lips move when making this sound. Notice whether you use the front, middle, or back of your mouth while making this sound.

This is a loud or (voiced) sound. Put your front teeth over your bottom lip. Use your voice and feel the vibrations. V tickles slightly when you say the v sound. Start to say valentine, but only say the first sound, and then stop. Don't put a vowel sound after the v.

On the student page:
- Emphasize that the letter looks like the object it represents.
- Find capital V on the Valentine picture and lower case v on the vase picture.
- Practice tracing the letter correctly using the correct strokes.
- Use large stiff arm strokes tracing the letter in the air.

Review when needed.

Encourage and praise efforts.

V v
consonant

Valentine

vase of violets

On Valentine's Day, Valerie Vee received a beautiful Valentine and a beautiful vase of violets from Vance. They watched a football game on t. v. Their team won the game. Valerie and Vance made the victory sign with their fingers. V for victory.

The word Vee is also the name of this letter.

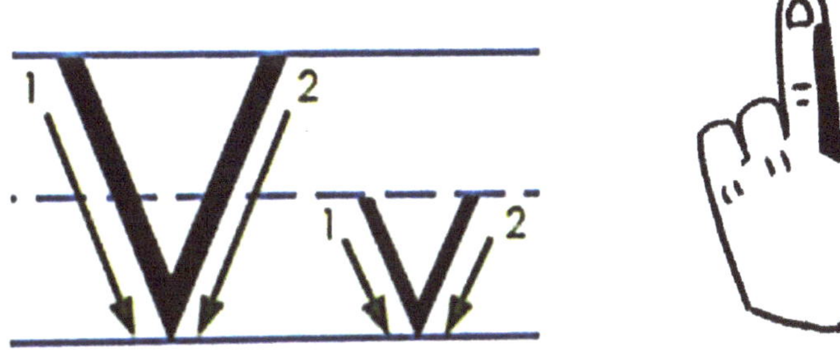

Capital V   lower case v

A B C D E F G H I J K L M N O P Q R S T U V W X Y Z
a b c d e f g h i j k l m n o p q r s t u v w x y z

W w
consonant

and sometimes acts as vowel for some ow words

Look in a mirror when you say the <u>w</u> sound to see how your mouth looks. Pay attention to how your tongue and lips move when making this sound. Notice whether you use the front, middle, or back of your mouth while making this sound.

When this letter acts as a <u>consonant</u>, it is a loud or (voiced) sound. Remember, don't put a vowel sound after the w sound.

<u>Vowel</u> sound for (o<u>w</u>) words: (o<u>w</u>) as a long vowel sound.

b<u>ow</u>
_ow sounds like the long o

On the student page:
- Emphasize that the letter looks like the object it represents.
- Find capital W on the Wagon & lower case w on the watermelon.
- Practice tracing the letter correctly using the correct strokes.
- Use large stiff arm strokes tracing the letter in the air.

W w
consonant

Wagon   **w**atermelon

Willie <u>W</u>. <u>W</u>alker was riding his wagon down the hills, when he heard his mom calling him to come home to eat watermelon slices. He rushed down the hills too quickly. Willie yelled, "<u>W</u>hoa wagon! Stop! <u>W</u>oe is me, if I turn over. I <u>w</u>ant to hurry, but not this fast!"

When you say the first sound in "<u>w</u>oe", you are making the w sound.

The word <u>w</u> sounds like it is double u. Double means 2 and <u>W</u> has 2 sides that are similar and connected.

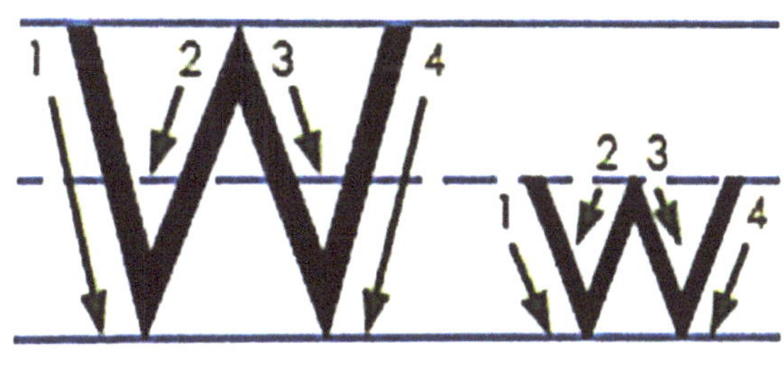

Capital W lower case w

A B C D E F G H I J K L M N O P Q R S T U V <u>W</u> X Y Z
a b c d e f g h i j k l m n o p q r s t u v <u>w</u> x y z

–X –x
consonant

Look in a mirror when you say the -x sound to see how your mouth looks.

Pay attention to see how your tongue and lips move when making this sound. Notice whether you use the front, middle, or back of your mouth while making this sound. X is usually an ending sound. A dash in front of the x, (-x), means it is in the final position of a word.

When x is the beginning letter of a word, it usually sounds like the z sound.

When x is an ending sound, you put your teeth together with your lips opened and make a hissing sound.

When x is the last letter of a word- "x sounds like ks together".

On the student page:
- Emphasize that the letter looks like the object it represents.
- Find capital X on the BOX picture. Find lower case x on the ax picture.
- Practice tracing the letter correctly using the correct strokes.
- Use large stiff arm strokes tracing the letter in the air.

**Look at an alphabet strip 1 letter at a time,
say the letter and its sound.**

—X —x
consonant
usually an ending sound

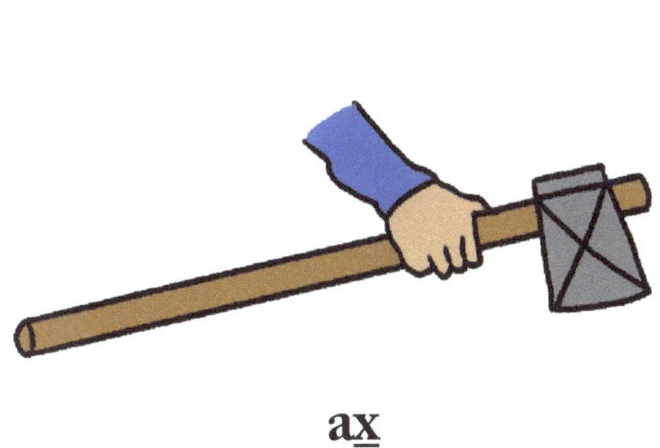

a<u>x</u>

BO<u>X</u>

Ma<u>x</u> could not open the big box.

He decided to use an a<u>x</u> to open the bo<u>x</u>. Ma<u>x</u> marked an <u>X</u> on the bo<u>x</u> for the spot to hit.

EXCEPTION: If <u>x</u> is used as the beginning sound, it usually sounds like a z sound.

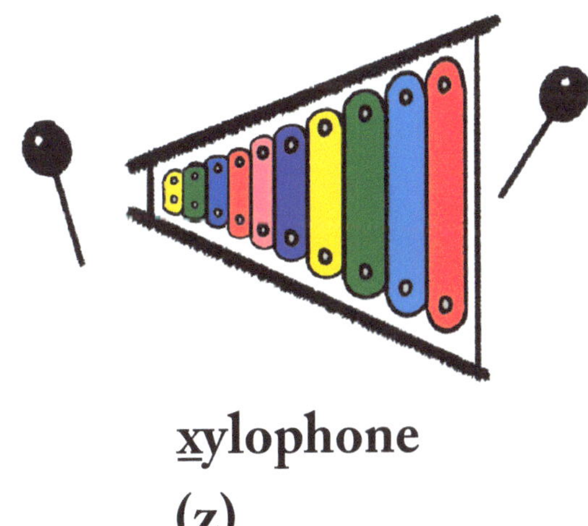

<u>x</u>ylophone
(z)

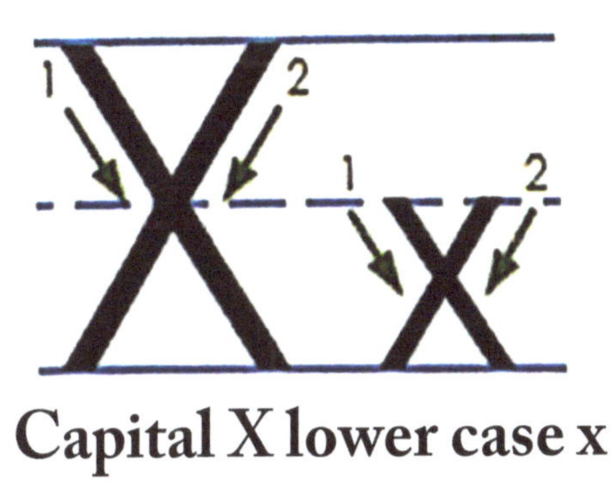

Capital X lower case x

A B C D E F G H I J K L M N O P Q R S T U V W <u>X</u> Y Z
a b c d e f g h i j k l m n o p q r s t u v w <u>x</u> y z

Y y
consonant

(and sometimes acts as a vowel)

Look in a mirror when you say the y sound to see how your mouth looks. Pay attention to how your tongue and lips move when making this sound. Notice whether you use the front, middle, or back of your mouth while making this sound.

When y is the first letter of a word, it usually acts as a consonant. Your mouth opens slightly when making this sound. Don't put a vowel sound after the y sound.

When y is the last letter of a word, it usually acts as a vowel. Y at the end of words says the long e (ē) or the long i (ī) sound.

EXAMPLES:

bunny
ē

fly
ī

On the student page:
- Emphasize that the letter looks like the object it represents.
- Find capital Y on Yolanda & lower case y on yarn and yo-yo.
- Practice tracing the letter correctly using the correct strokes.
- Use large stiff arm strokes tracing the letter in the air.

Y y
consonant
(and sometimes acts as a vowel)

**Yolanda
yawns**

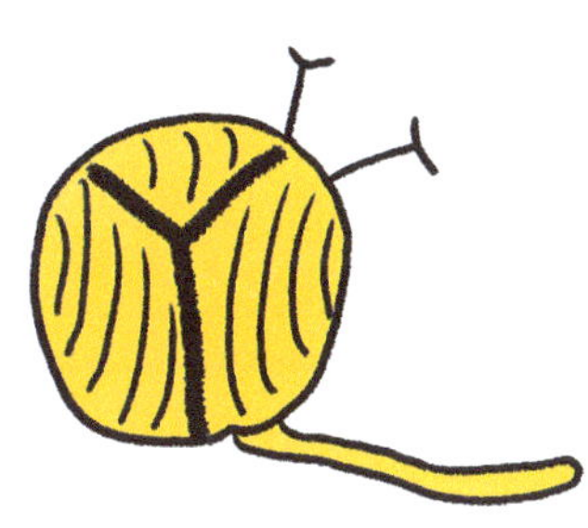

**Yellow
yarn**

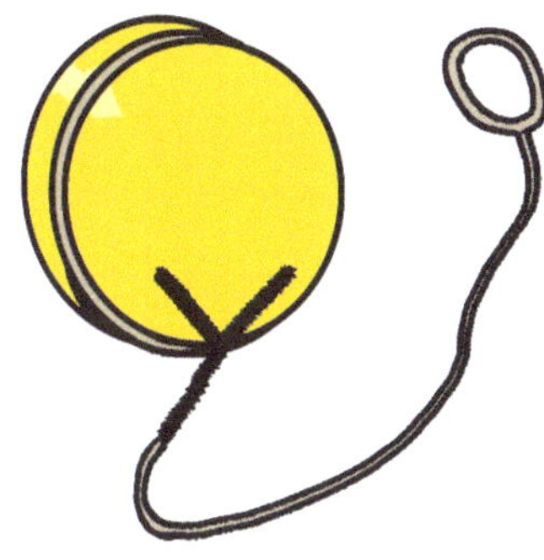

yo-yo

Yolanda was so sleepy that she yawned and grabbed the yellow yarn instead of her yo-yo. Yolanda found out that you can't yo-yo yarn. Yolanda cried, "Y-Y-Y!"

Ending -y acts as a vowel, -y at the end of words says:

**bunny
ē**

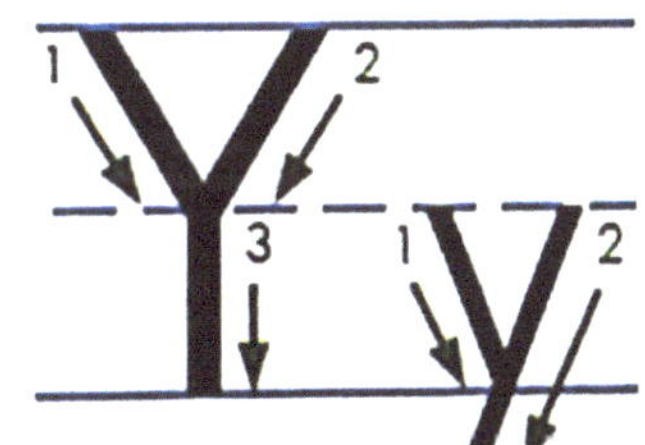

Capital Y lower case y

**or fly
ī**

A B C D E F G H I J K L M N O P Q R S T U V W X Y Z
a b c d e f g h i j k l m n o p q r s t u v w x y z

Z z
consonant

Look in a mirror when you say the z sound to see how your mouth looks. Pay attention to how your tongue and lips move when making this sound. Notice whether you use the front, middle, or back of your mouth while making this sound.

<u>Z</u> is a loud or (voiced) sound. The teeth are together when the buzzing sound of the <u>z</u> is made. Don't put a vowel sound after the <u>z</u> sound.

On the student page:
- Emphasize that the letter looks like the object it represents.
- Find capital Z on the Zebra picture. Find lower case z on the sound the bee makes when it buzzes z-z-z.
- Practice tracing the letter correctly using the correct strokes.
- Use large stiff arm strokes tracing the letter in the air.

Practice making the correct sound for all letters of the alphabet.

Z z
consonant

<u>Z</u>orro

A bee watched <u>Z</u>orro, the <u>z</u>ebra, at the <u>z</u>oo. The bee became surprised and started buzzing, "<u>z</u>-<u>z</u>-<u>z</u>!", when he saw what happened! <u>Z</u>orro looked like a <u>z</u>ebra until he unzipped the <u>z</u>ipper of his <u>z</u>ebra suit. A horse stepped from the <u>z</u>ebra suit. Now <u>Z</u>orro had <u>z</u>ero stripes. <u>Z</u>orro left the <u>z</u>oo to live on a ranch.

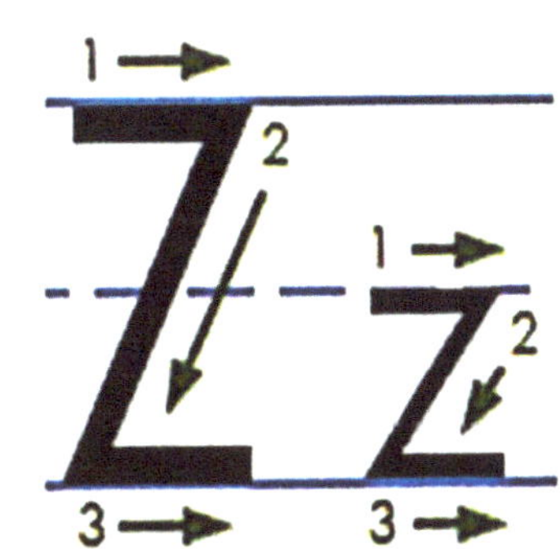

Capital Z lower case z

A B C D E F G H I J K L M N O P Q R S T U V W X Y <u>Z</u>
a b c d e f g h i j k l m n o p q r s t u v w x y <u>z</u>

www.ingramcontent.com/pod-product-compliance
Lightning Source LLC
Chambersburg PA
CBHW042043110726
48006CB00002B/276